PRINCEWILL LAGANG

Bound by Faith: A Christian Guide to Lasting Love

First published by PRINCEWILL LAGANG 2023

Copyright © 2023 by Princewill Lagang

All rights reserved. No part of this publication may be reproduced, stored or transmitted in any form or by any means, electronic, mechanical, photocopying, recording, scanning, or otherwise without written permission from the publisher. It is illegal to copy this book, post it to a website, or distribute it by any other means without permission.

Princewill Lagang asserts the moral right to be identified as the author of this work.

First edition

This book was professionally typeset on Reedsy.
Find out more at reedsy.com

Contents

1	The Foundation of Love	1
2	The Role of Faith in Love	4
3	Building a Strong Spiritual Foundation	7
4	Navigating Challenges with Grace	10
5	The Power of Forgiveness	13
6	Cultivating a Heart of Service	16
7	Nurturing Intimacy within Christian Values	19
8	Facing Life's Challenges with Grace	22
9	The Enduring Power of Faith	25
10	A Love That Truly Lasts	28
11	A Love that Inspires	31
12	Embracing the Journey Ahead	34

1

The Foundation of Love

It was a warm summer evening, and the sun was setting over the tranquil town of Graceville. The quaint streets were lined with charming, white-picket-fenced homes, and the fragrance of blooming flowers filled the air. In this idyllic setting, nestled deep within the heart of the Bible Belt, lived Sarah and Mark, a couple who were about to embark on a journey that would test the very essence of their love and faith.

For Sarah and Mark, faith was not just a Sunday ritual but the cornerstone of their relationship. They had met at their local church, Grace Community Fellowship, and their love had blossomed through shared values and a deep commitment to their Christian faith. Their relationship was built on the firm belief that love, when rooted in faith, could withstand any storm. This was the essence of their bond, and it was the foundation of this book.

As Christians, Sarah and Mark had encountered many challenges in their relationship. The inevitable struggles that come with life - financial hardships, the loss of loved ones, and personal disappointments - were amplified by the commitment they had made to each other before God. Their love had been tested time and again, and they had leaned on their faith to see them through.

In "Bound by Faith: A Christian Guide to Lasting Love," we will explore the profound connection between love and faith, and how these two pillars can strengthen and sustain a lasting, fulfilling relationship. Through the stories of Sarah and Mark, and the wisdom of countless other Christian couples, we will delve into the following:

1. The Role of Faith in Love: We will discuss the significance of faith in the foundation of a Christian relationship. How does faith shape our values, priorities, and perspective on love? What does it mean to walk in faith together as a couple?

2. Building a Strong Spiritual Foundation: The importance of grounding your relationship in prayer, scripture, and spiritual practices. How do daily devotions and shared prayer times enhance the bond between you and your partner?

3. Navigating Challenges with Grace: Relationships are not immune to trials and tribulations. We will explore how faith equips couples to face adversity with resilience and grace. What does it mean to endure hardships, sickness, and loss while keeping the flame of love burning?

4. The Power of Forgiveness: Forgiveness is an integral part of love. How can your faith guide you towards forgiveness and reconciliation in times of conflict and hurt?

5. Cultivating a Heart of Service: Love is not just about receiving; it is also about giving. We will discuss the role of selflessness and service in a Christian relationship, and how acts of kindness can strengthen the bonds of love.

6. Nurturing Intimacy within Christian Values: How can you maintain a passionate and intimate connection within the boundaries set by your faith? We will explore the art of intimacy and the importance of communication in a Christian relationship.

As we journey through the pages of this book, we will not only learn from Sarah and Mark's experiences but also draw wisdom from the Bible, theologians, and Christian relationship experts. Whether you are a newlywed couple, have been married for decades, or are still seeking the one with whom to share your faith, "Bound by Faith" is your guide to deepening your love and faith, and building a relationship that will last a lifetime.

In the following chapters, we will delve into each of these aspects, providing practical insights, real-life stories, and scriptural guidance to help you build a love that is truly bound by faith. Together, we will discover how the enduring power of Christian faith can strengthen the love between you and your partner, making it a love that truly lasts.

2

The Role of Faith in Love

In the serene town of Graceville, where faith and love intertwined like the vines of a well-tended garden, Sarah and Mark continued to be the embodiment of what it meant to be "Bound by Faith." Their love story had begun in the pews of Grace Community Fellowship, and their journey was a testament to the belief that faith plays a pivotal role in the foundation of lasting love.

As we delve deeper into this Christian guide to lasting love, we must first understand the integral role that faith plays in shaping the dynamics of a relationship. Faith is not simply a religious conviction; it is the lens through which we view the world, our values, and the guiding light of our lives. Within the context of love, faith serves as a compass, directing couples toward lasting love in several significant ways.

1. Shared Values and Priorities: In the book of Amos, it is written, "Can two walk together unless they are agreed?" (Amos 3:3). This verse speaks to the importance of shared values and priorities in any relationship. When a couple's faith aligns, it forms a solid foundation for their love. Christian couples often find harmony in their shared beliefs, which impact their choices, lifestyles, and the way they raise their families. Their faith becomes the guiding force behind every decision, providing clarity and unity in their

journey together.

2. A Covenant Before God: Christian marriage is not just a legal contract but a sacred covenant before God. The act of standing before an altar and exchanging vows, guided by faith, is a profound expression of commitment. This covenant deepens the sense of responsibility towards each other, creating a bond that extends beyond human understanding.

3. Strength in Unity: The Bible teaches that "a cord of three strands is not quickly broken" (Ecclesiastes 4:12). In Christian love, these three strands represent the union of two individuals and God. A couple's faith in God serves as the third strand, adding strength and resilience to their relationship. When challenges arise, as they invariably do, it is faith that binds them together, reinforcing their love and helping them withstand the storms of life.

4. Guidance from Scripture: The Bible provides guidance and wisdom for every aspect of life, including love. Couples who base their relationship on Christian principles and the teachings of the Bible often find a wellspring of wisdom to navigate the complexities of love. From passages that speak of love's attributes in 1 Corinthians 13 to the lessons of patience, kindness, and forgiveness, the Bible serves as a manual for Christian love.

5. Enduring Commitment: In Christian faith, love is not fleeting or conditional; it is enduring and selfless. A Christian couple's commitment to each other is deeply rooted in their belief in the eternal nature of love. They understand that love is not just a feeling, but a commitment to cherish and honor one another for a lifetime.

6. Prayer and Spiritual Growth: Prayer is a powerful tool in a Christian relationship. It allows couples to connect with God and with each other on a profound level. Prayer together can deepen their emotional and spiritual connection, fostering an environment of intimacy and trust.

As we navigate the role of faith in love, we must remember that faith is not a one-size-fits-all concept. Each Christian couple's journey is unique, and their faith will be expressed in their relationship in their own distinct way. This diversity is a testament to the beauty and depth of Christian love.

In the chapters that follow, we will explore practical ways to incorporate faith into your love story, including building a strong spiritual foundation, nurturing intimacy, and facing challenges with grace. We will also delve into the power of forgiveness and the importance of selfless service in the context of Christian love. Together, we will discover how faith strengthens the bond of love, making it truly lasting and enduring, even in the face of life's most challenging trials.

3

Building a Strong Spiritual Foundation

In the heart of Graceville, a town that embodied the ideals of faith and love, Sarah and Mark continued to be a shining example of what it means to be "Bound by Faith." Their journey was a testament to the belief that a strong spiritual foundation is essential for nurturing and sustaining lasting love in a Christian relationship.

In this chapter, we will explore the importance of building a strong spiritual foundation as a cornerstone of Christian love. This foundation encompasses daily practices, shared rituals, and a deep connection to God that strengthens the bond between couples, deepens their faith, and solidifies their love.

1. Daily Devotions: The Heart of Connection

Devotions are the heartbeat of a strong spiritual foundation. They are moments of connection and reflection, during which a couple comes together to read the Bible, pray, and seek guidance from God. Daily devotions provide a space for couples to share their thoughts, hopes, and concerns, fostering unity and intimacy.

2. Prayer: A Dialogue with God and Each Other

Prayer is a powerful tool for deepening spiritual connection within a Christian relationship. It allows couples to communicate with God and with each other in a way that transcends the ordinary. Praying together opens a window to each other's souls, creating a bond that goes beyond the physical and emotional.

3. Scripture as a Guide: Wisdom from the Word

The Bible is a rich source of wisdom and guidance for couples seeking to strengthen their spiritual foundation. The stories, parables, and teachings found within its pages offer insights into love, forgiveness, and the enduring nature of faith. Scripture serves as a guidepost, illuminating the path toward lasting love.

4. Shared Worship and Fellowship: Community Support

Worshipping together in a Christian community is an essential aspect of building a strong spiritual foundation. It provides couples with the opportunity to connect with like-minded individuals who share their faith, values, and aspirations. These connections offer a support network and a sense of belonging that can enhance a couple's love and faith.

5. Faithful Communication: Listening with Love

Effective communication is a key component of any lasting relationship. In a Christian love story, communication should be underpinned by the principles of faith. This means listening with empathy, understanding, and a desire to strengthen the bond between you and your partner. Communication becomes a vessel through which love and faith flow freely.

6. Emotional and Spiritual Growth: Nurturing Together

A strong spiritual foundation also fosters emotional and spiritual growth within a Christian relationship. As couples navigate life's challenges and joys, their shared faith provides a framework for personal development. They learn to support each other's growth, forging an unbreakable bond.

As we explore the concept of building a strong spiritual foundation, it's important to recognize that no two couples are alike. What works for one may not work for another. However, the underlying principle remains the same: faith is the cornerstone of lasting love. It provides a framework for daily living, a path to navigate life's challenges, and a source of deep connection and understanding between you and your partner.

In the chapters that follow, we will delve further into practical aspects of Christian love, including navigating challenges with grace, the power of forgiveness, and the importance of selfless service. We will explore the art of nurturing intimacy within Christian values and the role of faith in cultivating a love that endures. Together, we will discover how the enduring power of Christian faith can transform your love story into one that truly lasts a lifetime.

4

Navigating Challenges with Grace

In the peaceful town of Graceville, where faith and love walked hand in hand, Sarah and Mark were a living testament to the strength of a Christian love story. Their journey through life had not been without its trials, and in this chapter, we explore how their faith in God and their commitment to one another allowed them to navigate challenges with grace, emerging stronger and more united.

Every relationship, no matter how deeply rooted in faith, faces obstacles and tribulations. The key to enduring love is not in avoiding these challenges but in facing them head-on with the grace that faith provides. In this chapter, we will delve into the ways in which Christian couples can navigate challenges with grace:

1. Trusting God's Plan

Central to the Christian faith is the belief that God has a plan for our lives. Trusting in this plan can provide solace and perspective during difficult times. Sarah and Mark's story is a testament to this trust. When they encountered financial struggles, they turned to their faith, knowing that God's plan would guide them to a solution.

2. Turning to Prayer in Times of Need

Prayer is a source of strength and comfort in Christian relationships. In times of hardship, couples can come together in prayer, seeking guidance, support, and the strength to overcome challenges. This shared spiritual practice not only connects them with God but also deepens their emotional connection.

3. Encouraging Open and Honest Communication

Open and honest communication is vital when navigating difficulties in a relationship. By discussing their concerns, fears, and hopes with each other, couples can work together to find solutions. This communication should be marked by love, understanding, and a commitment to resolve issues with grace.

4. Respecting Each Other's Journey

As a Christian couple, you and your partner may have different ways of processing challenges. It's important to respect each other's individual journey of faith. While one might find solace in scripture and prayer, the other may seek guidance from a trusted mentor or therapist. Respecting these differences and supporting each other's unique paths is essential.

5. Forgiveness as a Healing Balm

Forgiveness is a cornerstone of Christian love. When challenges in the form of conflicts or misunderstandings arise, the ability to forgive is crucial. It's a way of extending grace to your partner and allowing healing to take place. Forgiveness doesn't condone wrongs but releases the hold of hurt and allows the relationship to mend.

6. Growing Through Adversity

In every challenge, there is an opportunity for growth. Sarah and Mark learned that adversity can be a catalyst for personal and relational development. By embracing trials as a means to strengthen their faith and love, they found the courage to face life's obstacles with grace and resilience.

Navigating challenges with grace is not about avoiding difficult times; it's about approaching them with faith and a commitment to your partner. As we continue to explore the journey of Christian love, remember that it's your faith, the bond you share, and your determination to face life's trials together that will ultimately define the enduring nature of your love.

In the chapters ahead, we will delve into more aspects of Christian love, including the power of forgiveness, the importance of selfless service, and the art of nurturing intimacy within Christian values. We will explore how faith strengthens the bonds of love and how, even in the face of adversity, your love story can truly last a lifetime.

5

The Power of Forgiveness

In the heart of Graceville, where faith and love intertwined like the roots of well-nurtured trees, Sarah and Mark had experienced firsthand the transformative power of forgiveness. Their love story was not immune to the trials and tribulations of life, but it was their unwavering commitment to forgiveness, rooted in their Christian faith, that had allowed their love to endure.

In this chapter, we explore the profound role that forgiveness plays in Christian relationships. Forgiveness is not merely a virtue but a pillar upon which lasting love is built. Here, we will delve into the following aspects of forgiveness:

1. Understanding Forgiveness in a Christian Context

In Christianity, forgiveness is a central theme. It is the act of pardoning others as God pardons us, and it aligns with the teachings of Jesus in the Bible. Forgiveness in a Christian relationship is not just about moving on from past wrongs; it's about showing the same love, grace, and mercy to your partner that God shows to you.

2. The Healing Power of Forgiveness

Forgiveness has a profound impact on emotional and spiritual healing. When a couple forgives each other, they release the burden of resentment and anger, making space for love, trust, and intimacy to flourish. Sarah and Mark's story is a testament to how forgiveness can mend even the deepest wounds.

3. Letting Go of Grudges and Resentment

Grudges and resentment are corrosive to a relationship. In a Christian love story, the commitment to forgiveness means letting go of these negative emotions. It's a choice to release the hurt and replace it with love, understanding, and compassion.

4. Seeking Forgiveness from God

Just as it's important to extend forgiveness to your partner, it's also important to seek forgiveness from God. Christian couples recognize that they are not perfect and may fall short of God's standards. Seeking God's forgiveness and grace enables them to continue growing in their faith and love.

5. The Art of Apology and Reconciliation

Apologizing is a humble act of acknowledging one's mistakes and seeking reconciliation. In a Christian relationship, apologizing is a way of demonstrating your commitment to your partner's well-being and the harmony of your love story.

6. The Cycle of Forgiveness

Forgiveness often becomes a cycle within a Christian relationship. When both partners commit to forgiving each other, the cycle perpetuates love, trust, and a sense of security. This continuous act of extending grace strengthens the bonds of their love.

As we explore the concept of forgiveness within Christian love, remember that it's not always easy. Forgiveness may require effort, patience, and humility. However, the rewards are immeasurable - a love that endures, a relationship that heals, and a faith that grows.

In the chapters that follow, we will continue to delve into practical aspects of Christian love, including the importance of selfless service, nurturing intimacy within Christian values, and facing life's challenges with grace. We will explore the enduring power of Christian faith in strengthening the bonds of love, making your love story one that truly lasts a lifetime.

6

Cultivating a Heart of Service

In the town of Graceville, where faith and love were intertwined like the branches of an ancient oak tree, Sarah and Mark continued to live out their love story as a shining example of what it means to be "Bound by Faith." Their journey had been one marked by selflessness, a commitment to serving one another, and a deep-rooted belief that love flourishes when cultivated with a heart of service.

In this chapter, we explore the significance of selfless service within a Christian relationship. Christian love goes beyond words; it is an active, living expression of love, driven by the example of Christ's selfless service. We will delve into the following aspects of cultivating a heart of service:

1. The Servant's Heart in Christian Love

Christian love is founded on the concept of servanthood, a notion deeply rooted in the teachings of Christ. Mark 10:45 reminds us, "For even the Son of Man came not to be served but to serve." In a Christian relationship, a servant's heart means prioritizing your partner's well-being, joy, and growth.

2. Acts of Kindness and Thoughtfulness

Small acts of kindness and thoughtfulness can make a significant difference in a Christian relationship. From preparing your partner's favorite meal to leaving encouraging notes, these gestures reflect the love and care you have for each other.

3. Sacrificial Love

Sacrificial love is the hallmark of Christian relationships. Just as Christ gave His life for humanity, Christian couples are called to make sacrifices for each other. Sacrifice is a testament to the depth of your love and your commitment to your partner's happiness.

4. Meeting Each Other's Needs

Understanding and fulfilling your partner's emotional, physical, and spiritual needs is an act of service. It requires attentiveness, empathy, and a willingness to invest time and effort into nurturing your relationship.

5. Service Beyond the Home

Christian love extends to service beyond the home. Serving in your local church or community can be a beautiful way to strengthen your love and faith as a couple. It reflects the belief that your love is not confined to your personal relationship but also reaches out to those in need.

6. Encouragement and Support

As a couple, you are each other's greatest cheerleaders. Encouraging and supporting your partner in their dreams and endeavors is an act of service. It is a way of demonstrating your belief in their potential and the importance of their aspirations.

Cultivating a heart of service within your Christian relationship requires a daily commitment to putting your partner's needs and happiness before your own. It is a conscious choice to emulate Christ's love and humility in your actions, both big and small.

As we explore the concept of selfless service within Christian love, remember that it is a reflection of your faith and a cornerstone of lasting love. It is the embodiment of the biblical commandment to love your neighbor as yourself, a principle that extends naturally to your partner.

In the chapters that follow, we will delve into more practical aspects of Christian love, including nurturing intimacy within Christian values, navigating challenges with grace, and the power of forgiveness. We will explore how faith strengthens the bonds of love and how, even in the face of life's challenges, your love story can truly last a lifetime.

7

Nurturing Intimacy within Christian Values

In the peaceful town of Graceville, where faith and love thrived in harmony, Sarah and Mark continued their journey as a testament to the power of Christian love. Their story exemplified the beauty of nurturing intimacy within the boundaries set by their faith, providing a model for Christian couples seeking to deepen their connection.

In this chapter, we explore the art of nurturing intimacy within Christian values. Intimacy is a vital component of any loving relationship, and in the context of Christian love, it is founded on the principles of faith, commitment, and mutual respect. Here, we will delve into the following aspects of nurturing intimacy:

1. Spiritual Intimacy

Christian couples often find that spiritual intimacy is a profound way to connect on a deeper level. This form of intimacy involves sharing one's faith journey, discussing spiritual insights, and growing together in faith. Regularly engaging in prayer and Bible study together can be a powerful way to foster spiritual intimacy.

2. Emotional Intimacy

Emotional intimacy is about opening up to your partner, sharing your feelings, thoughts, and vulnerabilities. It's the foundation for a strong connection, and Christian couples do this while guided by the principles of love, empathy, and compassion. It involves active listening, understanding, and offering support during times of emotional distress.

3. Physical Intimacy

Physical intimacy is an important component of any romantic relationship. In a Christian context, it is expressed with respect for the boundaries set by faith. It is a sacred act, reserved for the marriage covenant, and is a way to express love, affection, and unity between partners.

4. Communication as the Bridge to Intimacy

Effective communication is the bridge to all forms of intimacy. It is the means through which you express your love, share your experiences, and resolve conflicts. Open, honest, and respectful communication is essential for nurturing emotional, spiritual, and physical intimacy within Christian values.

5. Mutual Growth and Support

Nurturing intimacy is also about fostering mutual growth and support. Christian couples often find that they encourage each other's personal and spiritual development. They stand as partners in each other's journeys, offering guidance, understanding, and a loving presence.

6. Setting Boundaries with Love

In a Christian relationship, setting boundaries is an expression of love and respect. It allows partners to protect the sanctity of their relationship and maintain their commitment to God's principles. Boundaries can encompass physical, emotional, and spiritual aspects of intimacy, ensuring that they are in harmony with Christian values.

Intimacy within a Christian relationship is not merely about physical connection but the amalgamation of emotional, spiritual, and physical elements in a way that honors God and strengthens the bond between partners. It is a reflection of the love and grace you find in Christ's love for the Church.

As we explore the concept of nurturing intimacy within Christian values, remember that this form of closeness deepens your love, fosters unity, and allows you to experience the profound joy of love as designed by God.

In the chapters that follow, we will delve into more practical aspects of Christian love, including the importance of facing challenges with grace, the power of forgiveness, the role of selfless service, and the enduring power of faith. We will explore how, even in the face of life's challenges, your love story can truly last a lifetime.

8

Facing Life's Challenges with Grace

In the tranquil town of Graceville, where faith and love intertwined like the branches of ancient oaks, Sarah and Mark's love story was a living testament to the strength of Christian love. Their journey had seen its share of hardships, yet they faced life's challenges with grace, displaying a deep-rooted belief that their faith was the anchor that could weather any storm.

In this chapter, we delve into the profound art of facing life's challenges with grace within a Christian relationship. Adversities are an inevitable part of life, and in the context of Christian love, it's not about avoiding them but about responding to them with faith, resilience, and grace. Here, we will explore the following aspects:

1. Trusting God's Plan

Central to Christian faith is the belief that God has a purpose and plan for our lives, even in the face of adversity. Sarah and Mark understood that their faith was the bedrock of their relationship, providing them with guidance and perspective during difficult times. Trusting in God's plan allowed them to navigate challenges with unwavering hope.

2. Shared Prayer and Support

Christian couples often rely on the power of prayer and mutual support to face challenges. Praying together during difficult times provides comfort and connection, allowing both partners to draw strength from their shared faith. Mutual support involves being there for one another, offering a listening ear, and showing love in practical ways.

3. Perseverance and Resilience

Adversity tests the resilience of a relationship. Christian couples are often called upon to persevere through financial troubles, health issues, or other life challenges. Through faith and commitment to one another, they develop resilience that allows them to withstand life's storms.

4. Finding Meaning in Suffering

In the Christian worldview, suffering is not without purpose. It can be a means of spiritual growth and character development. Christian couples often find that challenges, when faced with faith, reveal profound insights and an opportunity for growth.

5. Forgiveness as a Healing Balm

In times of adversity, conflicts and misunderstandings may arise. Forgiveness is a key component of Christian love that allows healing and reconciliation to take place. It restores harmony within the relationship and provides a fresh start.

6. Growing Closer Through Challenges

Facing life's challenges with grace often leads to a closer, more resilient relationship. Adversity can strengthen the bonds of love and faith. Sarah and

Mark's journey attested to this, as they found that their shared trials served to unite them even more deeply.

Christian couples understand that challenges are not meant to weaken their love but to strengthen it. Their faith serves as a source of strength and guidance, allowing them to face difficulties with grace, dignity, and an unwavering belief that their love can endure.

As we explore the concept of facing life's challenges with grace within a Christian relationship, remember that it is not about avoiding adversity, but about growing through it. It is a testament to the enduring nature of faith and love.

In the chapters that follow, we will delve into more practical aspects of Christian love, including the power of forgiveness, the importance of selfless service, nurturing intimacy within Christian values, and the enduring power of faith. We will explore how, even in the face of life's challenges, your love story can truly last a lifetime.

9

The Enduring Power of Faith

In the serene town of Graceville, where faith and love flowed together like a gentle river, Sarah and Mark continued their journey as a beacon of what it means to be "Bound by Faith." Their love story had witnessed many trials, but it was their unwavering belief in the enduring power of faith that had guided them through the storms and illuminated their path.

In this chapter, we explore the profound role of faith in Christian relationships. Faith is not merely a set of beliefs but a dynamic force that shapes every aspect of a couple's journey. Within the context of Christian love, faith is the anchor that keeps love steady and allows it to weather the test of time. Here, we will delve into the following aspects of the enduring power of faith:

1. Faith as a Foundation

Faith is the bedrock upon which Christian love is built. It provides a solid foundation of shared values, principles, and priorities that guide a couple's life. With faith as their cornerstone, Sarah and Mark found a common purpose in their love and their commitment to God.

2. Weathering Life's Storms

Life is filled with storms—personal, financial, emotional, and spiritual. Christian couples understand that faith is the anchor that keeps them steady during these tempests. Faith provides the courage and hope to face adversity and emerge stronger on the other side.

3. The Role of Trust

Faith and trust go hand in hand. Christian couples learn to trust in God's plan and in each other. Trust is the bridge between faith and love, allowing a relationship to thrive with a sense of security and assurance.

4. Growth in Faith and Love

Adversity often presents an opportunity for spiritual and emotional growth. Christian couples find that their faith deepens through trials, allowing them to discover new dimensions of love and commitment. Challenges become stepping stones to a more profound connection with God and each other.

5. Faith in Every Season

Faith is not limited to the good times but is equally important during seasons of doubt, confusion, or grief. Christian love is resilient because it is rooted in faith that endures in all circumstances. Sarah and Mark's love story is a testament to this unwavering commitment.

6. The Fruit of Faith: Love That Lasts

In Christian relationships, faith bears fruit in the form of love that lasts. This enduring love is characterized by selflessness, forgiveness, sacrifice, and a commitment to cherish and honor one another for a lifetime. Faith nurtures a love that transcends the temporal and embraces the eternal.

Christian couples recognize that faith is not a passive element in their relationship but an active force that shapes their love story. It is the source of their strength, the light in their darkest moments, and the unwavering belief that their love can endure through all seasons of life.

As we explore the concept of the enduring power of faith within a Christian relationship, remember that faith is a living, dynamic element that requires nurturing and active participation. It is the key to a love story that stands the test of time.

In the chapters that follow, we will delve into more practical aspects of Christian love, including the importance of selfless service, nurturing intimacy within Christian values, facing life's challenges with grace, and the power of forgiveness. We will explore how, even in the face of life's challenges, your love story can truly last a lifetime.

10

A Love That Truly Lasts

In the picturesque town of Graceville, where faith and love intertwined like the roots of ancient oaks, Sarah and Mark's love story had been a living testament to the enduring power of Christian love. As we come to the final chapter of this guide, we reflect on the key lessons they embodied, and we strive to encapsulate the essence of a love that truly lasts.

In this concluding chapter, we explore the essential elements that define a love that stands the test of time, all bound by the unifying force of faith:

1. The Fusion of Faith and Love

The enduring love Sarah and Mark experienced was a result of the beautiful fusion of their faith and love. Their faith served as the guiding light, the moral compass, and the source of strength that fortified their love throughout their journey.

2. The Power of Commitment

Commitment is the bedrock of a lasting relationship. A love that truly lasts is one where both partners are unwavering in their commitment to each other and to God. This commitment fosters a sense of security, trust, and unity.

3. Nurturing Intimacy

Intimacy is a bridge that connects hearts. A love that truly lasts thrives on emotional, spiritual, and physical intimacy, all nurtured within the boundaries of Christian values. Intimacy is the language through which love is expressed.

4. Grace in the Face of Adversity

Adversity is an inevitable part of life. A love that stands the test of time is marked by the grace with which it faces life's challenges. Grace involves trust, resilience, forgiveness, and mutual support, all underpinned by faith.

5. Forgiveness as the Healing Balm

Forgiveness is the salve that heals the wounds of the heart. A love that truly lasts is one in which partners practice forgiveness, extending grace to each other, and making room for healing, reconciliation, and a fresh start.

6. Selfless Service and Sacrifice

Selfless service and sacrifice are at the heart of Christian love. A love that endures is one in which both partners put each other's needs ahead of their own, making sacrifices for the well-being and happiness of their loved one.

7. The Enduring Power of Faith

The unshakable faith that Sarah and Mark exhibited is the life force behind a love that truly lasts. Faith is the anchor in the storm, the unwavering trust in God's plan, and the source of hope in all circumstances.

In the concluding chapter of this guide, we find the essence of Christian love - a love that is deeply rooted in faith, commitment, and grace. It is a love that withstands the trials of life, grows through adversity, and transcends the limits of time. It is a love that not only endures but thrives, serving as a testament to the beauty of love bound by faith.

As you reflect on the wisdom and experiences of Sarah and Mark, remember that the path to lasting love in a Christian relationship is one that requires dedication, effort, and unwavering faith. It is a journey of self-discovery, mutual growth, and the profound realization that love, when rooted in faith, is a love that truly lasts.

11

A Love that Inspires

In the idyllic town of Graceville, where faith and love were woven together like a rich tapestry, Sarah and Mark's love story had become a beacon, illuminating the path for others on their journey toward enduring Christian love. As we embark on the final chapter of this guide, we explore the idea of a love that not only lasts but also inspires others to seek the same profound connection.

In this concluding chapter, we delve into the elements that make a love story truly inspirational:

1. Transparency and Authenticity

An inspiring love is marked by transparency and authenticity. Partners are unafraid to be their true selves, revealing their strengths and vulnerabilities. Their love story is honest, genuine, and a true reflection of their faith.

2. Embracing Imperfections

An inspiring love is not about perfection but about the beauty of imperfection. It celebrates the quirks, flaws, and differences in each partner, recognizing that it is these unique qualities that make their love story special.

3. The Power of Shared Values

Couples with an inspiring love share core values. Their love is rooted in their faith and beliefs, which serve as a foundation for their decisions, actions, and priorities. They live their values and inspire others to do the same.

4. A Relationship of Respect

Respect is the cornerstone of an inspiring love. Partners honor each other's autonomy, opinions, and boundaries. Their relationship is built on mutual respect, providing a model for healthy interactions.

5. Acts of Kindness and Service

Inspiring love is marked by selfless acts of kindness and service. Partners go out of their way to support each other, to care for their community, and to make a positive impact on the world around them.

6. Grace in Forgiveness

In an inspiring love, forgiveness is a way of life. Partners readily extend grace and seek reconciliation. Their willingness to forgive demonstrates the enduring power of their love and faith.

7. A Source of Encouragement

An inspiring love is an unwavering source of encouragement. It uplifts, motivates, and empowers partners to be the best versions of themselves. They are each other's greatest cheerleaders.

8. Sharing Their Journey

An inspiring love includes sharing their journey with others. Couples who have experienced the enduring power of Christian love often become mentors, guiding and supporting those who seek similar connections.

9. Leaving a Legacy of Love

An inspiring love has the potential to leave a legacy. It demonstrates that love rooted in faith can transcend time, and it encourages future generations to prioritize love, faith, and commitment in their own relationships.

As we conclude this guide, remember that your love story has the power to inspire and transform not only your own life but the lives of those around you. Sarah and Mark's journey serves as a testament to the enduring beauty of Christian love, a love that not only lasts but also inspires, uplifts, and motivates others to seek the same profound connection.

Your love, bound by faith, has the potential to be a shining example for others and to leave a lasting legacy of love that stands the test of time. May your love story inspire and empower those who are fortunate enough to witness its grace and beauty.

12

Embracing the Journey Ahead

In the charming town of Graceville, where faith and love danced harmoniously like a gentle breeze through the trees, Sarah and Mark's love story was a testament to the beauty of Christian love. They had shared their enduring love, offered guidance, and left behind a legacy of inspiration. In this final chapter, we embark on the journey ahead, exploring the notion of embracing the future with unwavering faith and love.

As we conclude this guide, we delve into the essential aspects of continuing to nurture and strengthen your Christian love:

1. Reflection and Gratitude

Take time to reflect on your journey. Express gratitude for the love you've shared, the challenges you've overcome, and the growth you've experienced together. Reflecting on your love story can deepen your appreciation for each other and God's guidance.

2. Setting New Goals

The journey of love never truly ends. Set new goals and aspirations for your relationship. Whether it's deepening your faith, nurturing your intimacy, or serving your community together, having shared goals can keep your love story vibrant.

3. Prioritizing Faith

As you embrace the future, continue to prioritize your faith. Your spiritual connection serves as a compass for your relationship. Maintain your daily devotions, shared prayer, and regular worship as a couple, allowing faith to be the guiding light in your journey ahead.

4. Strengthening Communication

Communication is the bridge that connects hearts. Continue to foster open, honest, and respectful communication. It's the key to understanding each other, resolving conflicts, and building a foundation of trust and intimacy.

5. Learning from Challenges

The challenges you've faced have been stepping stones to growth. As you move forward, remember the lessons learned from adversity. Use those experiences to fortify your love and faith.

6. Embracing Change and Growth

Life is ever-changing, and so is love. Embrace the changes and growth that come with it. Adapt to new phases in your relationship with faith, commitment, and love as your constant companions.

7. Passing on the Legacy

Your enduring love story has the potential to inspire and guide others. Consider mentoring younger couples, sharing your experiences, and leaving a legacy of love that continues to inspire and uplift those who seek similar connections.

8. A Love That Truly Lasts

Embracing the journey ahead means living a love that truly lasts. It's a love that endures through all seasons of life, transcending time and leaving a profound mark on the world.

As you continue your journey, remember that the path to lasting Christian love is an ongoing commitment. It's a journey of growth, discovery, and an unwavering belief in the power of faith and love. May your love story be a shining example, a source of inspiration, and a legacy of love that stands the test of time, leaving an indelible mark on your hearts and the hearts of those around you.

Book Summary: "Bound by Faith: A Christian Guide to Lasting Love"

"Bound by Faith" is a heartfelt and comprehensive guide to achieving enduring love within the framework of Christian values. In this illuminating book, the captivating love story of Sarah and Mark, residents of the serene town of Graceville, serves as a beacon of Christian love, guiding readers through the essential elements that foster deep and lasting connections.

The book unfolds through twelve insightful chapters, each one offering practical wisdom and real-life examples of how faith, commitment, and grace can fortify a loving relationship.

Chapter 1: The Foundation of Christian Love
   This chapter sets the stage by introducing the charming town of Graceville and the protagonists, Sarah and Mark. It emphasizes the importance of faith and commitment in Christian love.

Chapter 2: The Journey Begins

Sarah and Mark's love story unfolds in this chapter, detailing their initial meeting, the role of faith in their connection, and the foundation of their enduring love.

Chapter 3: Building a Strong Christian Relationship
The book explores the importance of trust, communication, and shared values in Christian relationships, all exemplified in Sarah and Mark's journey.

Chapter 4: Navigating Challenges with Grace
Readers are guided through the art of facing life's challenges with grace and faith, as demonstrated in Sarah and Mark's own experiences.

Chapter 5: The Power of Forgiveness
Forgiveness is explored as a cornerstone of Christian love, with real-life examples of how Sarah and Mark's relationship was strengthened through forgiveness.

Chapter 6: Cultivating a Heart of Service
The book delves into the significance of selfless service within Christian relationships, illustrating how service and sacrifice can nurture love.

Chapter 7: Nurturing Intimacy within Christian Values
This chapter explores the art of nurturing emotional, spiritual, and physical intimacy within the boundaries of Christian values, using Sarah and Mark's story as a guide.

Chapter 8: Facing Life's Challenges with Grace
Adversity is examined as a testing ground for love and faith, with Sarah and Mark's unwavering commitment to each other and their shared beliefs as the foundation for facing challenges with grace.

Chapter 9: The Enduring Power of Faith
The enduring nature of faith is explored, illustrating how it serves as an

anchor, guiding light, and source of strength in Christian love.

Chapter 10: A Love That Truly Lasts

The essence of a love that stands the test of time is unraveled, highlighting transparency, embracing imperfections, respect, and service as core elements.

Chapter 11: A Love that Inspires

The book explains how a love story can be not only enduring but also inspiring, leaving a legacy that motivates others to seek similar profound connections.

Chapter 12: Embracing the Journey Ahead

The concluding chapter provides guidance for embracing the future, maintaining faith, setting new goals, and continuing to strengthen your relationship as you navigate the journey of enduring love.

"Bound by Faith" is a touching guide for Christian couples seeking to deepen their love, faith, and commitment. Through the compelling love story of Sarah and Mark, readers gain valuable insights and practical advice to build a love that endures through all of life's challenges and joys, leaving a lasting legacy of faith and love.

www.ingramcontent.com/pod-product-compliance
Lightning Source LLC
LaVergne TN
LVHW021054100526
838202LV00083B/5972